Bruce William Fraser

WORDS TO INSPIRE

Copyright © 2011 by Bruce William Fraser

All rights reserved. Neither this publication nor any part of this publication may be reproduced or transmitted in any form or by any means, electronic or mechanical, including photocopying, recording or any information storage and retrieval system, without permission in writing from the author.

ISBN: 978-1-77069-267-1

Word Alive Press
131 Cordite Road, Winnipeg, MB R3W 1S1
www.wordalivepress.ca

Library and Archives Canada Cataloguing in Publication

Fraser, Bruce William, 1928-
    Words to inspire / Bruce William Fraser.

Poems.

ISBN 978-1-77069-267-1

    I. Title.

PS8611.R365W57 2011   C811'.6   C2011-901685-0

Dedication

This collection of poems is dedicated to my friend, Robin Lynn Noftall of Vancouver, whose help, inspiration and encouragement contributed greatly to the writing and the production of the poems.

The collection is also dedicated to my children, Martha and Stephen.

Contents

Part 1: Poems of Inspiration   1

Part 2: Life, Love, Friends and Family   29

Part 3: Travel Observations   51

Part 4: Poems on Various Subjects   69

Part 1

Poems of Inspiration

Searching for Answers   3

Creation and Saviour of the World   4

My Prayer   5

My Angel   6

An Angel   7

The Test   8

The Samaritan   9

Bartimus   10

Freedom for Women   12

Good Friday   14

Easter   16

Words to Inspire

Thanksgiving Day 17

Christmas 19

Angels on Earth 21

Angel of Death 23

A Father's Love 24

Thanks Be to God 26

Searching for Answers

Why is it?
We look for treasures in strange surroundings
Putting our faith in persons unknown to us
Hoping to find some miracle,
That our lives may be fulfilled.

Millions of people
Searching for their individual "Peace",
Seeking a stranger who may have the answers
To solve their problems,
Stimulating their existence in so many ways.

White cane in hand
We pass by signs and situations,
Missing the chance to share our life
With those who love us most,
Accepting far less than we deserve.

Where is the power
To catch and hold the jewels of great value?
The ability to see what stands before us,
Offering to enrich our very being
Making us alive with purpose and with love.

Awaken we must
While life embraces our every living act
To the joy and purpose of our troubled lives
Guiding us to the place we ought to be
Enjoying life, before we breathe our last.

In God we live
And move and have our being,
As we receive His body in the Mass
Our lives, refreshed, reach forth to do His will
And blessings flow, with promise of Salvation.

Creation and Saviour of the World

The creation of the world was an act of Love, set in time
Before life had appeared in this clime.
Water and rocks were fixed in their place,
Providing a site with large areas of space.
Valleys and mountains were formed in their beauty,
Rivers and lakes, to exist for their duty.
By the power of creation, the world was made,
An act of Creator, whose works were displayed.

Only a God could perceive such a plan
Then he acted to populate, with woman and man,
Animals added, completed the scene
Wild and domestic, some loving, some mean,
Cattle and sheep, for the uses of man.
Fruit trees and gardens for food in the land
Water, to wash, and to use for Baptism,
A means to bring all men into his mission.

Paradise lasted, until man was tempted,
To turn against God, made his status "exempted",
Who was this God that ruled over man?
We reasoned, without Him, we will do what we can,

Then God looked down from His heaven above.
"To save man from himself, I must show him my Love"
A baby was born, to this confused world he came,
God living as man, but not searching for fame.

He came healing and teaching, Jesus, Son of God
Facing crowds of people, wherever he trod,
He knew he must die, to save man forever,
A sacrifice for the sins of man, a plan so clever,
His last act, to die on a cross made of wood,
Like a criminal, offered to save those He could.
When Jesus rose from the dead on the third day they knew
'twas the Lord God of Heaven, come for me and for you.
Now the path to eternity lies open before us,
We should praise God together and join in the chorus.

My Prayer

O Lord, that lookest sadly down,
Upon thy world, plunged deep in strife
Help us to struggle through out plight,
Reveal to us Thy Son this night
And guide us to a nobler life.

Thou gavest us a beauteous land,
So like Thy heaven, in which to dwell
Gay fluttering leaf, tall stately pine.
Sweet singing bird, fruit on the vine,
That we might praise and love Thee well.

Look deep into our hearts, and hold
The Face of thy dear Christ before our eyes.
Make our blind errors, light upon our mind.
Give to us Grace, the truth of thy dear Son to find
Not only in Thy house, or in the skies.

The prayer of all that cry to Thee for help
Is that we might abide in harmony
One with another, leaving pride and wealth
In Christ our Saviour, we can find our health
We give our strength, our soul, our all, to Thee.

My Angel

When I least expected,
God sent an Angel into my life,
Changing everything that went before
Making the future new and exciting.

United in Spirit we forge ahead,
Each in our separate corner of the world,
Remembering the blessings we share
Thanking our Father for His Love.

The strength of the Almighty,
Binds us in a bond,
Seeking to share the joys
Of special friendship, that endures.

Whatever comes, we will survive
Knowing our love, God has ordained
Will provide us power, for daily activities,
Determination to overcome the evil one.

As we proceed in life, separated only by distance,
Memories will sustain our friendship for each other
Raising our hears in prayer and thanksgiving
For our Heavenly Father Who has brought us together
Our God of Love who died, and lives to give us Peace.

An Angel

Everyone should have
An Angel like you in their life.
A sincere and true friend,
You lift me up when my spirit is low,
Your kindness and love touch my soul.
When I would have given up,
You came into my life and revived me
You have shared my joys and my sorrows,
You accepted me, as part of your life,
My cup overflows.
Your faults are so minimal, your potential unlimited,
Through you I am blessed.
I sense the Holy Spirit working through you
Everyday I thank our Lord in Heaven for You.
Everyone needs an Angel in their life.
My Angel is unique, a very special soul.
No one will ever come close to taking her place.
A beautiful, loving, caring Child of God.

The Test

There came a day, from many years gone by,
That God and Satan came to face each other.
A test of Love and strength was set between the two.
God showed his trust in one He loved named Job,
Who lived his life, devoted to his Lord.
Satan threw out the challenge, to turn this man,
Until he would come to curse his Lord and lose his faith.

The plan was to take away the wealth, comfort and love
Known to the man throughout his life till now,
Leaving him desolate, defeated, in pain, with no support.
The Lord said to Satan, "Behold he is in your hand."
Then Satan, filled with hate, began control of the servant of God
Causing such suffering, as man could not imagine.
Bereft of all the comforts he had ever known.

Job sat in the ashes, body covered in boils, all joy of life gone,
Rejected by family, his wife suggesting he renounce God and die.
Friends came to comfort him, but gave no real help
Depression filled his mind, as he cried out in pain, for relief
Calling on God, to overcome his painful state.
No help was given, yet he did not blame his Lord,
Looking within himself to find the reason for his torture.

This was a test, unknown to Job, overseen by his Lord.
As Satan tried in vain to break the spirit of this man

Having no success, against a strong willed believer.
Finally, the tide turned, as God reached down
To bless his faithful servant, rewarding his devotion.
Restoration was made to increase every aspect of his life
Proving the bond of faith, stronger than any evil force.

How often in life is man tested by forces of evil?
Powers of darkness reach out to hold us in their grasp
Man came to earth formed of clay, in the image of God
With purpose on our journey, to reflect the Love of our Creator,
Formed with imperfections, facing daily innocent temptations.
We seek reward meant to be given to all men living,
Who, rejecting evil, walk in faith and love with our living Lord.

The Samaritan

The Road from Jerusalem to Jericho,
Was often a crime scene, with many unsavory people,
Lying in wait, to rob and injure unsuspecting travelers.
On one such occasion, a man was brutally attacked
Beaten, naked and robbed of clothing and all possessions.
He lay in a ditch, suffering, close to the point of death.

Many people passed by, unwilling to get involved.
A priest crossed the road to avoid the scene.
One of the temple staff, touched by his curiosity,
Stopped to see what happened, then hurried on his way.

Only a stranger, passing through the country, stopped,
Showing concern; he helped the injured man to survive.

The man from Samaria, was not expected to show kindness
Only his inner goodness urged him to do what was right.
He gave support, binding wounds, taking him to a hotel
Paying for someone to look after the suffering man,
An act of neighbourly humanity in an unforgiving world,
Providing loving care, for one of God's children.

Who is my neighbour? The question rings in our ears.
Could it be a person I owe for services rendered?
We may think only of those living in close proximity to us.
The answer may differ for those who care to ask.
Real neighbours are those kind, loving people who help,
Like the Samaritan, seeking no reward for self.
Willing to share our burdens, as we travel in God's world.

Bartimus

His name was Bartimus; a beggar
Doomed to depend, on others for his food
As, daily, he sat by the side of the highway,
Hearing the passers-by, but seeing nothing.
Many years of darkness, had been his fate
The son of Timaeus, blind from early days,
Calling to those who passed, for help to survive.

One day, the sound of many voices arose,
Giving him hope, that help was on it's way.

He knew not what, the cause of the commotion,
As the crowd approached his chosen place to beg.
He listened and heard the name of one mentioned;
A teacher and healer, travelling through the land,
They called him Jesus, bringing hope to many.

Bartimus cried out in desperation, "Jesus, son of David
Have mercy on me".People shouted at him, "Keep your peace".
But, the blind, dependent man cried all the louder;
"Please!Son of David, have mercy on me".
Then Jesus stopped, turning to the man.He called him to come near.
Compassion showed as he enquired, "What do you want of me"?
Bartimus, in faith pleaded that he might receive his sight.

Strong hope and trust were shown, in his request,
Believing the power of healing, could be given.
Jesus was moved by the faith of this blind man.
With love and understanding, He said,
"Go your way your faith has made you whole".
Bartimus opened his eyes, finding his sight restored.

Modern blindness restricts our vision of love and beauty in this world,
Like Bartimus, many struggle daily, to find their way,
Neglecting the truth that God reveals to man.
One well marked path, will lead mankind to his promised home,

Taken by the teacher, offering his life for our wrongs, on a cross of shame.
The words to life clearly written for our understanding, "I am the way"
Giving sight to those blind of truths, set down by our Creator.

If we would seek to find the way for man to reach his eternal reward,
We, like Bartimus must call on the son of David, in prayer.
For He, the teacher, was in reality the Son of God, building His kingdom,
One with God in the beginning, coming as a man to live among us.
Death on a cross for our sins, leaving a priesthood to lead us to Him
Providing a means to share in His life, to receive His Body, His Blood.
A way, through our living Lord, to obtain the gift of eternal Love.

Freedom for Women

Her name was Mary, a gentle woman,
A child of God forced by her determination to survive,
Walking the streets of Jerusalem, selling herself,
To those who wanted her, only to satisfy their own desires
Facing experiences, of abuse, unloved by any.
A face troubled by sadness and circumstance.
Her body, bearing the marks of violent living.

Her trade was hidden from the crowds around,
Known, but unknown, by most who sought her service
Until, one day, she was discovered by chance,
Involved in what she did, to make her living,
Taken to the open court beside the temple,
Accusations made; requiring laws to be applied.
The cry from all the crowd rose high "Stone her. Stone her"

The sentence fit the crime.Men who had abused her,
Felt no shame; She had to pay the price of crime.
At that very moment, one appeared, a teacher preaching Love,
Followed by many, seeking his powers and teaching,
Arriving in their city, on his travels.He saw the situation,
Looking in the eyes of the woman, he saw a child of God,
Mistreated, yet no worse that her accusers.

He spoke with authority, as they carefully chose their stones
"You, who are free from any sin, throw the first stone"
The crowd was shocked by these words of wisdom,
Their thoughts turned to the sins they had hidden for so long
Then, one by one, they dropped the stones, walking away in silence.
As Mary bowed her head, in thanks for her deliverance,
Seeing accusers gone.He turned to Mary and said,
"Neither do I accuse you; Go and sin no more."

Two thousand years have passed since that day.
Yet women are still enslaved by men who have no love,

Showing their love to men, who only show rejection
Forgetting that men and women were created to be equals.
Domination of women still exists for many souls.
Persons like Mary, seeking independence not respected.
Unequal pay, for the same work, divides man and woman
Modern forms of suppression, designed to favor man.

The Love that Jesus showed to Mary
Presents a model for everyone on earth.
Happiness will only come to those who show mutual respect
Accepting the rights of co-workers and of mates.
Bringing no accusations, examining imperfections in their lives
Not ready to cast the first stone, at one, they say, they love.
We can live in peace, only if we so desire.

Good Friday

On a hill named Golgotha (the place of the Skull)
A bright sunny morn, outside Jerusalem.
A crowd slowly gathered to witness a sentence carried out.
Soldiers from Rome, marching up the hill,
With a man, full of sorrow, they were ordered to kill.

They knew not the reason the man was condemned,
Yet they joined in their act to the very end,
Nailing his body to a cross made of wood.
Raising it up, on the ground where they stood,
Completing their task, as directed, they should.

As the man, on the cross, began slowly to die,
The soldiers threw dice for what they could not buy
The clothing of one, who would suffer his fate,
Providing a chance to make gain from this act,
Without giving thought, to question the fact.

The crowd standing near, were shocked by the sight,
They had seen only Love in this man, it wasn't right.
Mother and followers, fearing loss of the plan,
They had thought He would rise to be King of the Jews,
Now his life ebbing out, they felt pain at the news.

The heavens joined in, darkness was seen,
As the earth acknowledged the loss of their teacher,
Who had blessed many lives as a merciful preacher,
Healing the sick, forgiving sins, raising the dead,
A spear pieced his side, and his body bled.

Three hours of pain, unlike any other,
Rejected by man, abandoned by father,
"Why", he cried, "Have you forsaken me"
While the crowd jeered, tempting him to show his power
To become their true Messiah, in his final hour.

A final moment, as life swiftly passed,
An empty body only, remained, at last,
Taken, for final resting, placed in the tomb of a friend,
A kingdom hoped for, appeared to be denied,
The crowd of friends, in mourning, left his side.

A Roman centurion, contemplating the events,
Witnessed that day, was touched in his heart,
Understanding, he said "Surely this was the Son of God"
His statement would be remembered for centuries to come
As he revealed the truth, about the Blessed One.

Times has passed and we, the children of God, give praise,
For the Sacrifice made, on the cross, to pay the price,
That was due for all the sins of mankind, willingly offered.
Christ died, Christ is Risen, Christ lives forever.
Thanks be to God, Blessed Father, forever Amen.

Easter

To all who choose to listen.
The words sound, loud and clear,
The Lord who came from heaven
Lives on, in lives of men and women here
To bless our lives, direct our paces,
Giving Love, reflected in our faces.

The Holy Child of Bethlehem,
Matured to teach and lead all men,
Understanding our place in God's creation.
Our right to inherit His salvation
For the one who came to lead our nation
Gave His own life that we might live,
And share eternity, that only He can give.

On Easter Day the proof was given,
No power on earth, can touch His heaven.
As souls baptized we share it all,
Unless we choose, in sin, to fall.
The choice is our eternal decision,
To suffer Hell, or share the joy of heaven,
For God so loved us, that He came,
To bear the cross, and take the blame,
For our imperfect acts of shame.

Let our hearts give thanks this day,
That Jesus chose the price to pay.
To free us all from harm and sin,
He opened heaven's gates to let us in.
Christ the Lord is Risen, indeed!
Let no man show hate or greet
But open wide your heart to God,
Whose many Blessings make us proud.
Alleluia!Christ is Risen! Alleluia!

Thanksgiving Day

Thanksgiving Day is a time of joy.
Enjoyed by every girl and boy
A family event of coming together
To savour the harvest and autumn weather.
Turkeys and pumpkins take their place,
A delicious gift, for the human race,
Thanks to our Father in heaven above
Whose blessings each day, express His deep Love.

We may be unworthy of all we receive,
His gifts are eternal, for all who believe,
When man had sinned and fallen away,
He came to this earth, our ransom to pay,
By teaching, he showed us the right paths to choose,
We find all the truth in His book of Good News.
To atone for our weakness, He was nailed to a cross,
While the world hardly knew, they had suffered a loss.
As his life slowly ebbed, blood poured from His side,
Committing His soul to His father, he gave up and died.
One Roman soldier, who stood near on that sod,
Was heard to say "Surely this man was the Son of God".
Risen, on the third day, he assured us, to know
That He would be with us wherever we go,
As the centuries pass, our debts of thanks increase,
For many brave souls, sacrificing life for peace.
Marching to war, to contain evil men,
Our soldiers defend us, determined to win.
The efforts of many, have brought us our peace,
With trust and assurance, our fears are released.
While places on earth, still constricted by strife,
As evil forces strive to deprive them of life.
We have been spared from much suffering and loss
Led by the God/man who hung on the cross,
So lift up your hearts, and thank our Living God today,
For life, friends, love and safety, we gratefully say,
Thanks to all, God and Friends, for this wonderful day.

Christmas

What kind of world do we live in today?
As some share in luxury, the poor fade away.
Wars and poverty cause misery, in places
Stress and discomfort is seen on men's faces.
To a world not much better, the Holy Child came,
His mission determined, to suffer in shame.
Like a lamb to the slaughter, for those bound by sin
On a cross, life was offered, their forgiveness to win.

Today powers of evil, have risen to new heights.
Days filled with terror, gangs roaming by night.
Guns used by youths, with no feelings for others,
Killing the innocent, who could be their brothers.
Brave men with purpose, march off to war,
Where rockets and road bombs, attempt to kill more.
Life seems to have lost its sacred position
As more men neglect to honour God's mission.

Church bells ring out, calling faithful to Mass,
Celebration of events, from centuries past
When shepherds, in fields outside Bethlehem,
Were summoned by Angels, to the Saviour of men.
In a stable so humble, with a manger, His bed,
The Christ child lay sleeping, free of all dread.
While outside the city, led by a star
Three kings came to worship, from places afar.

Words to Inspire

The birth of God's Son, by prophets foretold,
Took place in a stable, as shelter from the cold.
As the animals, quietly watched, standing by,
Mother Mary gave birth, and heard the child cry.
A voice that would some day give hope to all living
Inspiring the nations, by His promises giving.
Hope, Love and Peace to those who would hear,
A message eternal, remembered each year.

As church bells ring out, the Gospel proclaimed,
The intentions of God are embraced and maintained
While daily, the blessings of God to man come,
Our hearts are enriched by the teaching of the Holy One.
At Christmas, the hopes of mankind are fulfilled,
The Kingdom of God, on this earth we must build,
By embracing kind acts, with the love God has given,
We, in our lifetime, will strive to reach Heaven.

All the presents and kindness that we receive
Remind us of Blessings, for all who believe.
Each year Christmas wakes us to thinking of others,
Sharing love with our siblings, Fathers and Mothers.
The joy of the season, refreshes our life,
To face a New Year, free from worry and strife.
So enjoy the festivities, as long as they last
God is with us forever, when Christmas is past.

MERRY CHRISTMAS!

Angels on Earth

As the cold days of winter, hit the streets of Toronto,
A homeless man with only worn and tattered clothing
To fend of the icy blasts sat, seeking his daily bread.
With threadbare clothing tightly wrapped around;
His hat lay before him, to catch any pennies offered,
With future uncertain, a victim of circumstance,
Before the recession, his life showed certain promise.
Today, his unshaved face, downcast eyes, bottle ready,
His life, lacked promise, weighed down by fear and doubt.

A dapper young man, on his way to business,
Dropped a loonie in the hat and said "Seen any angels lately"?
"Not bloody likely. Ain't any in this world", the man replied.
With downcast eyes hoping others would also see his need.
But at that moment, a spark flashed, awakening memories
Of better days, when life was not a struggle to exist,
And future hopes had filled his heart, a time when Angels
Seemed to mean so much.

This desperate soul searched his memory, and he recalled,
The teaching of his youth, when the angel Gabriel came to Mary
Proclaiming God's Plan to save mankind, "She would conceive.
And bear a Son in Bethlehem who would grow to be the Savior
Of this world, changing all things to fulfill His Father's wish".
A light shone, in the heart of this poor man,
And his rebirth to a better life began. A sign beckoned him,

With help to those whose life had lost its way "Yonge Street
  Mission"
He read, and crossed the street to re-enter the life he left
  behind.

Seeing the need of this disheveled soul, they offered to help
  with food,
Clothing, and a vision of what might be. Their acts of love
  and kindness
Made a serious impression on this sad person, opening
  immense possibility,
Now shaved and better clothed, renewed in spirit, he
  ventured forth
Fear gone, he found employment and a new life began.

Years quickly pass as life reaches to find new goals.
One day the man returned, to visit his old neighborhood.
On the corner where he had sat, another took his place,
He thought of the stranger, who had stopped to help, so
  long ago.
Looking around he spied that same man and asked "Do you
  recall
Meeting me"?The man replied "I've never seen you before"
Then the man confessed that he had been asked by this man,
"Have you seen any angels lately?" "Today I can answer that
  question".

"I have seen many and YOU are the angel, who gave me
  back my life
When Kindness without price, is freely given.Our acts make
  us His Angels.

Far from Heaven, by acting for our God, that His Will may be done.
Angels appear unknown to us, in many ways with support and love.
To all, who knowing God are blessed, and also to those who know Him not
God's Special Angels come to show His Love and give Him praise.

Angel of Death

The Angel of death came down from Heaven
To gather the souls that God had given,
From those whose lives, their bodies had left,
Mourned by friends, families feeling bereft.
Of the ones they thought, would last forever
But fate finally caught them, the weak and the clever
Planning their lives to develop and grow
Unaware of their future, but how could they know?
Babies lives ended, by means they could not fight,
Termination to life at all ages, it didn't seem right.
Some were determined to choose their own fate,
To work towards a future, they just couldn't wait.
Terror and mayhem on roads accounted for others
Sisters and mothers, children, fathers and brothers,
Disease and accident claimed many a soul,
War in its brutal form, took away the most bold.
To engage in a conflict, with hopes for world peace.
Some fell victims to warfare, providing no ease.

The Angel was touched by the numbers he saw,
As he worked, gathering souls, he was in awe
The total was large, so many lives spent
More to be added, wherever he went.
Then he thought of the loss to His Father above
Each soul so precious, in His Father's Love.
He considered the blessings, awaiting their arrival
Knowing His Father would have care for them all.
New beginnings awaited the souls who reached Heaven
The sins and mistakes of the past were forgiven
Our moment of death has been hid from our eyes,
We never will know, no matter how wise.
So our task here on earth is to adhere to God's way
Until the day comes, the Angel takes us away.
When we labour in Love that our goals be fulfilled,
We leave the quest for others to continue to build.

A Father's Love

Two boys were born to a prosperous man
Who worked hard to help him wherever they can
Facts were established, they were his Heirs
Their future secured, they made choice without fears.
The eldest spent his life caring for his legacy
While the younger son chose a life of ecstasy.

Collecting his share, he departed his home,
Looking for pleasures among those who roam,
Hard days lay ahead as his lessons he learned
The value of pleasure, would have to be earned.

In short time his "friends" and his money were gone
Used for selfish wants, no plans for later on.

Reduced to his lowest state, he thought of his father
Regretting his action and sinking even farther
He decided to return and ask for employ
On the land which had been half his when he was a boy,
Pleading forgiveness for all he had done
Ashamed of his past, he had lost and not won.

When his father saw him, his heart leaped for joy
He could only think of his loss of his boy.
He saw the occasion as a time to celebrate
His lost boy was home, life would be great.
While out in the field, elder brother worked on his own
And resented the fact that his brother was home.

He watched his young brother, being treated like royalty
By father, who had never given him such a joyful day.
Taken for granted, his jealousy grew
He could not share the joy that his father knew
How many times, the events of this story are told
Youths today eagerly search for their goals as of old.

Many go seeking fortunes; some led by temptation
Choosing wrong paths, with no emancipation
When they come to their senses, and return to their home,
Father is waiting, His love to be shown,
So too, when we stray from the ways of our Lord
He awaits to forgive us and take us aboard.

His love was first shown when He died for our sins,
Opening the door to Heaven for us to come in.
The roads lie before us, our choices to make
To walk with our Lord, or our own path to take.
Whatever we choose, we are still in God's sight,
He's watching to see us make choices for right.

When our life is complete and we stand before our Lord
Our record will show if we lived by his Word.

Thanks Be to God

I thank you Lord when I awake,
For all you've given to make life great.
For strength to work and time to rest,
Friends and family, the very best.
For dreams and future hopes ahead,
That spur us on, new roads to tread.
For skills obtained by trial and study
To make us for our tasks most ready.

I thank you lord for little things,
Spiders and bugs and bees with stings
Each with a purpose designed for life
Doing their thing as they see right.
For fish in the seas and animals on land
Each having a purpose as You command,
Food for the hungry and pets for our company
Working together as a fine tuned symphony.

We give our thanks, we raise our praise,
Your plans provide, for all our days.
'Tis sad to think of those who do not hear
Don't know our Lord, as one we hold so dear.
His love is ever with us to the end.
Our Lord, protector and our special friend.

Part 2

LIFE, LOVE, FRIENDS AND FAMILY

I Love You   31

Lost Love   32

The Journey   33

The Family   34

The Beginning of Life   35

The Miracle of Life   36

Mothers   37

Babies Rule   38

Love Trilogy #1 — Love Lost   39

Love Trilogy #2 — Love Found   40

Love Trilogy #3 — True Love   41

My Special Friend 42

Distance and Togetherness 43

Action of an Observer 44

To a Friend of Value 45

Meeting By Chance 46

A Meeting of Strangers 47

Telephone Call from a Friend 48

Best Friends 49

I Love You

Three little words, so important to hear
Expression of thought, a sentiment so dear,
Of all the words that make the world right
"I love you" mean most, a cause to excite.
For a heart that needs comfort and needs to know
That someone out there, their feelings will show.
Inner thoughts turned to words, mean a great deal
To the desolate and lonely, it improves how they feel.

In life we so often assume things understood
While the world that surrounds us, makes it hard to conclude
Close friends must know that we love them for sure,
Their constant reminder in words, show they care.
But the words spoken yesterday, are part of the past
We need constant reminder that their love will last.
It lifts us from darkness to light when we know
That the love shown today, for tomorrow will grow.

No matter what happens, on our journey through life,
Disappointments, arguments, experiences of strife.
Family upsets, money problems, that cause deep unrest,
Can only be conquered, when we're at our best.
We need reassurance, that love is still living
A word from a friend or our mate is worth giving.
For our love for each other will continue to grow,
As we tell them we love them, they surely will know.

Lost Love

The rain is falling gently,
For the day has come to rest.
As the night, like somber shadow
Stands to guard the world at peace
But my heart is filled with sorrow
And my soul with trouble pressed
For the love I cherished solely
Has insisted on release.

God hath given us noble mountains,
Beauteous flowers, birds and trees.
Now to me these all seem shapeless
For there's naught as sweet as she.
I can see her now in memory,
Pure in heart, child of the free
But alas I ne'er can hold her.
She is gone fore'er from me.

The hours are dragging forward
When the time will come to wake.
For me the lights are growing dim,
Since that last life-spark she break
But as earth persists through hazards
And as rivers reach the sea
So, my light will be rekindled
And a new world cast for me.

The Journey

Two roads led into a dark forest
Far separated by time and space,
Leading to many unknown places and adventures,
Designed to test everyone who chose to enter,
They twisted and turned, over hills and valleys.

A man and woman ventured onto these roads,
Each taking separate paths to reach their goal,
Not knowing where the trip ahead would lead;
Unaware of the experiences they would encounter,
Blindly seeking answers to their hopes in life.

Years passed slowly, as the road took turns,
Providing moments, good and bad to each
Presenting countless times of joy and sorrow,
Light and darkness, shaping their lives on the road
As they searched and sought, they knew not what.

One day, the roads converged and they met,
Two lanes became one, to emerge from the forest.
At their meeting, two lives found common purpose.
The journey had tested them with all the trials of life.
Now together, they walked boldly into their future.

The life they shared, proved the journey a success.
When asked to be his wife, she answered "yes".
The world stood still as love controlled the time.
Vows made, a new chapter of their life began.
Thanks to the roads that led them to this place.

The Family

Two people start a journey in life,
A man with resolve soon finds a wife.
They two join together, according to plan,
Sharing their lives, loving each other,
Preparing their future, as father and mother
A miracle works, as a new life began.

The family is shaped by arrival of child,
Sharing in creation, by an action so mild.
Life quickly changes, as small babies grow,
To become active toddlers, always on the go.
Years fly by as child reached their youth,
Confusing their parents, seeking the truth.

Families expand, when new siblings arrive,
Former plans change, now a task to survive.
Dreams and goals of members often conflict
Choices once easy become difficult to pick.
To function together requires strict devotion
As ships charting course, on a crowded ocean.

Large families present unsolvable challenge,
To keep all order, someone has to manage.
Personalities clash as individual goals appear.
Separation by age can cause many fears.
Disappointment, frustration, leading to tears,
Problems of dysfunction can last many years.

When journey begun leads to lifetime of bliss
Unexpected blessings can be easy to miss.
Respect for each other, a hug and a kiss
Cementing relations, love shared by everyone,
Reveals the plan of creation, for man not to fall,
As God, in His Heaven, pours His Love on us all.

The Beginning of Life

Life begins! It's starting time,
We may not know
A small murmur, from deep inside
Our self, like a humming bird,
Begins to flutter, and the miracle
Becomes Reality.

Sometimes we are surprised.
By life implanted, and growing
In our bodies
We find results of our actions
That awaken us to the Truth of Nature.
God's creative process, meets our needs.

Time passes, sickness is soon forgot,
As the thrill of anticipation
Controls our thought, and fills our heart with joy.
The future may seem impossible
But we, who embark on such a journey
Give praise to God, when the miracle is complete.

The Miracle of Life

One tiny sperm travels to woman from man,
Perhaps by surprise, more likely by plan
Seeking an egg, to join in embrace.
Feeling near lost, in this dark, fluid place,
Spying a target, the sperm latches on,
Catching the moment, before it is gone.
Together they join to begin their new life
Days of easy growth, causing bodily strife.
Nausea in mornings, indicating a sign,
Something working inside, a difficult time.
Confirmed by a test, the future foretold
New life would arrive, to be part of their fold.
Man and woman, thrilled by the thought
Would soon be sharing, whatever they got.
Mystery clouded the future event,
A child in the family would make them content,
Months of development, slowly take place,
Event approaching, increase for the human race.
Planning and saving, to prepare for new life,
Concern and excitement for husband and wife.
When time has progressed to the moment of birth
Pain grips the woman, like nothing on earth
The moment is tense, but the process begun
Brings results, most positive for everyone.
A new baby rests in its mothers' arms
While father smiles down, on all of her charms.
The journey has ended, the miracle done
Together, love shared with their blessed one.

Life, Love, Friends and Family

Life having potential for future success,
Begins a new journey, to grow and impress
From humble beginnings, we reach for the stars
If intentions are right, then the future is ours
Joining with all in the eternal plan
We are led to succeed, be it woman or man
Be strong in resolve, heroic and bold
In our final moment, our story is told.

Mothers

Of all the people across the land
Mothers are first to offer a helping hand.
Conditioned to care, and treat their child with love,
Like Angels, they have special powers from above.
In pain and joy, they watch their babies grow,
Waiting for their birth, when they will show.
As boys or girls, as they begin this life,
Adding to mother's constant strife
A child and a husband to care for now.
They feel the pressure, as wondering how
The tasks of living will all get done
Shared by two, but mostly by one.
Feeding and bathing baby, meals to prepare
Washing clothes daily, to provide proper care.
Out for walks in the cool fresh day,
Shopping for three, more bills to pay.
Meeting with doctors, sharing with mothers,
Family and friends, little time for others.
Children develop as strong boys and girls,

Mothers delight to see their whirls.
Before years have passed, the babes become adults
Learning new ways, in a world filled with cults,
Religion, sports and studies, so much to be done,
It's a wonder they have time to have any fun.
While mother's concerned that their children will grow,
To choose the right paths, wherever they go,
Most of her worries stem from her own early life,
While exploring, adventures, before becoming a wife.
Praying, their future, be honest and true
When facing unknowns, they will know the right things to do.
So mother gives thanks for the life of her child,
Whenever she sees her little one smile
For the path she had chosen, more loving than any other,
Her hope for the future, to become a grandmother.

Babies Rule

On the streets of the city
Couples stroll in the evening,
Pushing their strollers with baby aboard
Their lives now controlled,
By duties for their little one,
When a cry is heard, they stop,
Checking their child, feeling in charge,
But baby is really the one who controls.

Any sound from the stroller
Gains their instant attention

Bottles for food, soothers to pacify
Mother's open arms to offer their love
Safety and comfort, a daily requirement
Providing for child a healthy start in life.
All demands met, all needs fulfilled,
The child becomes a vital social being.

Parents are proud to display their prodigy,
Taking the credit for one they have borne
While under the surface, the mind of the baby
Holds knowledge that they're really in charge
Starting from early days, working their plan,
To have all adults bow to their command.
When parents think that they have done it all,
Baby shrieks, and knows they're in control

Love Trilogy #1 — Love Lost

When love flies out the window,
Two hearts are touched by pain.
The bond that held them for so long
Will n'er be seen again.
Their life, which seemed determined
To last, till end of time,
Now shattered into pieces
While only in its prime.

As memories fade, new friends appear.
The love that was, seems not so dear
Adventure comes to all who seek,

New love creeps into lives once more,
When we provide an open door
A lonely heart seeks love from someone new,
The search is what one really needs to do.

We were not meant to live a life alone.
Our quest will surely lead us to our mate
Where life becomes a joy, and not our fate.
For, two hearts beating to the tune of one,
Is the intention, when love has begun.
Past journeys from our memory fade away
As new love comes to us, as come it may.

Love Trilogy #2 — Love Found

What is Love? And where does it appear?
In the eyes of an infant, loved by its mother
From family closeness, sister to brother.
Girls staring at boys, in classroom so bright
Man seeking woman, in darkness of night.
Animals, sharing the company of others,
Beings striving to share in creation
Joining together in Love found relations.

The laws of the universe speak to our mind,
That life may continue, a mate we must find.
No matter what part of the world we inhabit,
The drive to produce, will keep us alive.
We live in a world ruled by forces of Love
Direction clearly given to us from above

Thus life will continue, as long as we find
Another to join us, in like frame of mind.

Love can be noticed in all of creation
The beauty in Nature, respect for our Nation,
Smiles from friends, kind words spoken,
Hearts restored to life, in bodies near broken.
Some seeking perfection appear to be blind
To the needs, all around them, so easy to find.
Love, sharing with others should be our prime task,
For love freely given, returns more than we ask.

Love Trilogy #3 — True Love

The greatest love that man can see
Is given, without a thought of me
Declared in acts, to please another
Son or daughter, friend or brother.
Central in our mind, showing a real devotion
Makes life complete, like ships on a calm ocean.

Time is required for love to take its place,
Based on knowledge, determined to face
A future, which includes the one so loved.
Resolved to live in peace together,
In spite of disagreement, or stormy weather,
As a ship sails proudly to the shore,
So lives desire, to please each other, more.

When two resigned to live and love as one
Their new life, blessed with joy, has just begun.
Children arrive to join this happy scene,
With smiles and laughter such as not has been.
Without true love and sharing of devotion
Forming a family is like a ship on a stormy ocean.
Love must be sufficient, that every need by met
A loving, caring future then is set.

The beauty of true love, is in its being.
It fills the heart with warm and tender feeling
The bond is formed, so permanent and strong
That nothing can give cause, to make things wrong
A unity of mind and bodies found
The future built as bricks, on solid ground
Formed to withstand, the worst that life can give.
Success and happiness, as long as they shall live.

My Special Friend

My special friend, from far away,
I met upon a train, one day,
With hair of gold and sparkling eyes,
Her beauty took me by surprise.
My inner soul, awoke in me
And said, "a friend of yours she'll be".

Time passes, allowing us to know,
Our friendship might begin to grow.
Contact, provided knowledge such,

That closeness helped us both so much.
We talked, and found that we could share
A friendship built on trust and care.

The months pass, and change appears,
A new man met her needs of years.
Blessings would come, with a little child,
Her hopes fulfilled, God, on them, smiled.
Yet still the first friendship will grow
By sharing all we need to know.

Spiritual love from sister and brother,
Can bind and satisfy one another
Special friends, mean so much in life.
Health and happiness, freedom from strife
As day and years pass, leaving us behind,
A lasting friend, is often, our most special find.

Distance and Togetherness

Our days on this earth may seem short,
But life can be eternal
The miles may separate us
But our friendship continues on,
Surely it has been blessed, by the eternal God.

Bodies settled in two distant cities,
Spirits, joined by eternal Love.
Nothing can really separate
Those who share strong, mutual feelings
Melded by the Power of the Almighty One.

Paths often lead to new adventures,
Determined by the events of the moment.
A time may come, we know not when,
That distance felt may disappear
A time for togetherness may come to be.

Whether in this world, or in the next,
Destiny often leads to states unknown.
Our hopes are answered through prayer and Love,
By our God who cares for us daily,
So may our future meet His Plan.

Action of an Observer

The elderly man had settled in his comfortable chair,
His eyes gazing around at the people out there,
When an event, cross the road, showed a scene of despair
A young child had been left alone in a car.
It's mother didn't know, that one watched from afar,
Planning to steal the car and depart, quickly away.
When the mother looked up, it was too late to act,
Her child and car gone, she awoke to the fact,
She had left the car running, to keep her child warm,
But her act of compassion, had left him to harm,
The old man acted quickly, cell phoned the police,
Reported the robbery, told all the pertinent facts.
With his help, the culprit was caught in his acts.
The child was returned to it's desperate mother,
In tears for her action, causing pain for herself and others.
She embraced her found child and vowed, never again

Would she leave him alone, it had caused so much pain.
The elderly man relaxed in his chair,
Feeling good to have helped, seeing the child now in care.
No one would know of his call to police,
He insisted, his efforts would not be released.
The mother gave thanks to the Lord up above,
As she hugged her sweet child, and gave him her love.
So often good intentions will lead to regret
We need full awareness, when our plans are set.
Knowing morals of some, strive to destroy the good life
By crimes they commit, with guns or with knife.
Many thanks to observers who act in their haste,
When foul acts are transpiring, there's no time to waste.
Together we share the work of controlling crime
To dispel need for worry, we seek Peace in our time.

To a Friend of Value

A good friend always, brings peace to my heart
Whether together, or miles apart
Making the night like day, when sunshine comes
To warm our lives, as friendship has begun.
Before we met, life seemed so drear and dark,
Without direction, like an empty park,
Where one might enter, totally alone
A journey where the end could not be known.
Life in its time needs moments that excite,
For the day when friendship will appear as right.
Such is the case, when two meet one day
To share their secrets, as they feel that way.

New life begins as fear is put to flight
A soul once doomed begins to see the light
The future, once uncertain, gains new sight.
When friends feel safe to confide in each other
A bond is forged, much like sister and brother.
Care and concern part of the equation,
Two spirits joined, forming a strong liaison.
As days and years so quickly pass
The joys of friendship yet will last,
Until days end and time to pass will come.
My life has been enriched, you are the one
Who made life better, in so many ways.
I'll thank my God for you, on all my days.

Meeting By Chance

Out of the night, she came,
A vision of special beauty
Troubled by past events,
Seeking peace and order in her life.

By chance, she met a stranger,
Sharing parts of her troubled past.
Her caring, loving, attitude
Began a friendship stronger than she could know.

Her life revived, working in a new field,
Having potential to reach the stars,
Which, applied, led to success among her peers
Taking life in a totally new direction.

Returning to her once strong faith,
She found the strength that God alone can give,
Like bamboo, she grew to greater heights,
The pride of her family, and her stranger/friend.

In life we often feel all alone,
But God sends His Spirit through others,
To lift our hearts in joy and praise to Him.
Then Peace comes, with understanding, to our hearts.

A Meeting of Strangers

One day, the paths of two persons met by chance,
Man and woman, having different goals.
She, a striking young woman, with many talents.
Hardly realizing her true potential or her beauty
He, an elderly man, facing final moments,
Having lived a busy life, with an uncertain future.
Upon these two the light of Heaven shone down
And suddenly they knew, that God had intended
A friendship to begin.

Each looked to other and was amazed, that some
Unknown power was pulling them together.
A mutual feeling, that could not be overlooked.
Slowly, over many moons, the friendship grew,
Like a mighty bamboo tree it reached Heaven,
And God looked down, and in His deepest Love
Blessed this unlikely union of two spirits,
Bound in love and friendship for each other.

Life is very hard to understand.
At times we enjoy all the pleasures of this world,
Not understanding that our actions are ruled by a
Higher power, who directs our moves on this stage
Creating situations for our life to grow.
Talents and potentials will be used for benefit to all.
Age will not prevent new goals to be reached.
God will act, to make all things come to be.

Telephone Call from a Friend

The telephone rang and you were there.
Lighting up this dull world of mine
Like the aurora borealis shimmering in the northern sky
Or fireworks, exploding to brighten the darkness
Your star shone into my life.

You spoke and a thousand twinkling bells
Sound in my head, stimulating my senses
Warm and embracing as a tropic breeze
Sparkling like water in sunlight down a rocky stream

The words are not important, but the tone of your voice
Suggests a love that cares, feelings so sincere.
Like father and son; mother and child
A sense of knowing that endures beyond all trials.
It streams into my soul and gives me peace.

Too soon the call is ended, silence returns.
Memory takes over to relive the pleasant moments past.

The robins return to find the nest they built last summer,
Lovers stroll again the paths where they found ecstasy
And my heart thrills, recalling your words once more.

Best Friends

Of all good things, God does provide,
The best is a friend, to stand by our side
When grief or sorrow take joy from our life
Best friends help to lift our burden of strife.

Knowing that, out there, is someone who cares
Who will rescue us from the suffering we bear,
That makes our life difficult, increasing our stress,
There's a friend to help us cope with our mess.

The bond that exists between friends will grow,
Respect for each other, gives peace that we know,
Love and care freely shown, sharing in prayer
Positive goals set for rejecting despair.

When the sun shines bright, in a sky crystal blue,
Friends often appear who profess to be true
Willing to share when the weather is fair
But when dark clouds come, they are gone, to where?

When pressure smothers us, no relief is in sight,
The friend who is true, lends resource to our plight,
A smile, helping hand, offers welcome relief,
We are lifted from doom, and relieved of our grief.

As we journey in life we may find roads that bend
On our pilgrimage, we may suddenly meet a new friend
We know not God's purpose, in setting the scene
A stranger appears one never before seen.

God provides us with one, to lighten our load,
Who supports and encourages us to walk down this road,
A best friend develops as our relationship grows,
With love and care to sustain us wherever we go.

Thanks be to Creator, who rules all of life
Who cares for our needs, and assists us through strife
Who sends us a friend when our needs reach their height
That we have someone close to our heart ,day and night.

Part 3

TRAVEL OBSERVATIONS

Barrie in February   53

Vancouver (B.C.) in March   54

Bottles and Cans   55

Rome   55

Glacier Bay   56

London (England)   57

Halifax   58

The Clothesline   59

Toronto Airport   60

Berlin   61

The Polar Bear Express   62

The Canadian   64

Afternoon in English Bay (B.C.)   66

Winter in Moose Factory (James Bay) 1946   67

Barrie in February

Softly, the flakes come down from heaven,
Touching the trees, the roofs, the drifts of snow
Which had arrived, some time ago.
Winter, in its frozen beauty,
Ready to welcome, each new speck of snow,
Like babies nestling in their mother's arms.

The Bay, where children swim and play,
Is quiet, lined with fishing huts
Taking their place, until the warm winds blow
Patches of solid ice appear.
Roads are difficult to travel
All eyes are searching, for a sign of Spring.

Each season has its purpose,
As the earth moves, ever closer to the sun.
The cold and severity of the winter breezes,
Will soon give way to changes in our lives,
Birds will return, to give us serenade,
As trees and flowers burst with life again.

Perhaps, we fail to understand,
The Plan that rules our universe.
We have four seasons to enjoy,
Each with its beauty and distinctive mode.
Variety has been our special journey in life,
Thanks to our Creator, for His gifts to man.

Vancouver (B.C.) in March

The cold winds blow.
Shaking the trees, where eagles nest, in Stanley Park
On the shores of the great Pacific.
Snow and rain, touches the treetops
Settling on mountains, rising round about.
March, roaring like an angry lion,
Stirring the ocean, covering land with soft white blanket
Causing birds and flowers to stay their course,
Until the warmth of springtime will appear.

Buds on branches, shoots in gardens,
Struggle to enrich the earth, with natural beauty.
Parts of creation surging to be seen.
Shades of green invade the grass.
As sun grows stronger, days are longer,
Changing patterns, in our world.
As Spring creeps quietly into view,
Like a kitten, softly stepping into an unknown place
So, life renews itself in many ways.

The cold dark days of winter,
Begin to beat a quick retreat.
As if a new age has begun
The signs of spring repeat.
The robins come to build their nest,
Animals of every kind are seen, ready
To raise a family of their own kind.
Young men and women, filled with love

As they join together in acts of creation.
Canada will grow, a much stronger Nation.

Bottles and Cans

While resting on a bench by the shore of English Bay
Observing the many ships, that come from far away,
Sunshine beaming on all the souls present,
A scene to be treasured, and never resented.

When down the path comes a disheveled man,
With a large bag stopping at each garbage can.
His quest, to recover bottles and cans,
Making his living, as best he is able,
By doing the things of which he is capable.

Passing by quickly, he seeks his next target
Filling his bag with things others forget
Our thoughts soon dismiss him, out of sight,
As we gaze at the scenes that give us delight.

Rome

In the ancient land of Italy
The city of Rome shines like a beacon,
Ruled by the mighty Caesars,
A Kingdom which at that time was the centre of the world
Crosses were raised on the hills round the city
Those who disagreed with Caesar were sent to death.
Some ended up in the coliseum, to battle hungry lions,

A sport enjoyed by the emperor, no doubt who won.
Bodies were laid in the catacombs, outside the city
To this day their bones remain in the underground passages.

A section of the city holds the Vatican
Centre of the religious worship, home to the leader
Papas to the Catholic Church in the world.
The Bishop of Rome, elected Pope by the Cardinals
To control the function of Spirituality of the whole Church
Men of great Faith and Love for all of God's people
Chosen to fill the sacred office as leader of the Church
Buildings filled with treasures, art, paintings and statues,
Representing the best of the Italian artist.
A tribute to Rome, and an offering to our Heavenly Father.

Glacier Bay

In the beautiful land of Alaska,
You may discover a very small bay
Fed from above by a river of ice
That flows down the mountain that way.
In the midst of a wilderness,
With mountains surrounded,
No buildings are found, only birds in the sky,
Weaving and gliding, as o'er it they fly.
Such beauty and silence, leave visitors astounded,
Gazing at icebergs and chunks floating by,
Cruise ships arrive, turn slowly around,
So all can observe, this marvel of Nature.
Water turned green, from ice grinding stone ,

TRAVEL OBSERVATIONS

It moves down the mountain, as a live creature,
Crawling slowly, toward its final zone.
One can only imagine, how lonely it gets
When the winds and the snow bring their icy blast
The visitors all have departed at last.
So, we leave with regret, return, never we may,
To the avalanche mountain in Glacier Bay.

London (England)

Of all the cities in England, London takes the crown.
Steeped in history, a royal centre of a town.
Perched on the banks of River Thames
Its bridges lead to other ends,
The home of Queen Elizabeth, who rules
Her palace secure from stranger and fools.
No finer place these is to visit,
You don't agree, tell me where is it?

The Globe where Shakespeare gave us plays,
Studied by students even today,
The tower of London, with the jewels, so rare
Collected by Monarchs while ruling with care.
Big Ben ever showing the time of day
Crowds off to Canary Wharf, their time to play.
Busses with upstairs, a quaint place to ride
Harrods for shopping, if the prices are right.

Hyde Park with speakers, on soapboxes posed,
With personal messages, presented so bold.

Theaters playing the latest of shows, like
"Broadway in New York", a city with hype.
A visit to London offers more than we can guess.
If an offer to go there is given, you should say yes
No city on earth has more options to share.
I can tell you no more, you have to be there.

Halifax

Fast changing weather greets the visitor,
To this well established, coastal city
Built on steep hills leading down to the harbour.
Few signs remain today, of the tragedies,
Suffered by many, from the storms and war.

High on the rise , overlooking the area,
Stands the Citadel, firmly built, a fort of protection
For the city and the harbour below,
A veritable fortification of yester year
Built to keep invaders from Canada's shore.

The time on one clock does not change,
Stopped at the moment when explosives reigned
Killing many, an accident, destroyed much of the harbour.
A moment in time, etched forever in memories of survivors
Today, a new vibrant city has risen from the ashes of the past.

A day of cold driving rain, followed by a warm sunny day,
Time to walk around to appreciate the beauty of the city.
Maritime Museum, displayed items from the Titanic, also

Stories of other ships lost, of proud men who fished the Atlantic,
Revealing some of the early history of our Nation.

On leaving the city, one feels the pride of being Canadian
Having a better understanding of days when Canada was young
Halifax was the cradle of the nation, brave men and women landed here
To settle land, reaching to the Pacific and north to Hudson's Bay
With unlimited potential, a land of the free, for all who would be Canadians.

The Clothesline

As the train sped north from Halifax,
It drew near the bustling city of Truro.
Many buildings flashed by the windows,
As slowly, we approached the station.
Attractive houses, presenting a pleasing landscape
Then, eyes were drawn to a clothesline,
Stretching from an upstairs window, reaching,
To join a building at the end of a long backyard
Loaded with clothing, drying in the open air.
Such a sight is rarely seen in our age of technology,
Electric dryers have risen to take over the task.
In many places today outdoor lines are not permitted
Community rules prohibit anything unpleasing to the eye
Yet the vision of a family's clothing, hung out to dry

Was a refreshing sight to those who have lived through
Changes in social habit, memories of long ago.
Before the days of modern means, clotheslines were normal,
In Summer, the soft breezes blew past, removing
The moisture from the clothes, giving them a sweet smell.
In Winter, ice formed on sheets and shirts,
Brought in frozen they hung on racks around the stove.
No one would have considered an electric dryer.
The scene in Truro is a real reminder of an age, now past
When life was more simple and far less expensive.
Our clean clothes have lost the sweet smell of outdoors,
From an age where clotheslines were a vital part of life.

Toronto Airport

Bustling crowds, leaving for far away places,
Carefully checked, by Airport security,
Determined to carry out their inspections.
All luggage, coats, canes, metal objects, x-rayed.
Having passed through this intensive check
They gather in pods to await their flight.

Rows of seats filled with weary travelers,
Destinations to parts of Canada and the world.
Two women, waiting to fly to Labrador,
Large numbers, seeking to reach Vancouver.

Time drags on; it seems to take forever,
As more appear, with like goals in their plan.
Opened bags reveal preparation by some.

Travel Observations

Food in small packages give comfort to the traveler.
Chocolate and chips, meeting needs of nervous people.

The crowd increases, until one asks "Is there room
For the many lining up with excess baggage."
Finally the call comes, to board our plane.
Large numbers walk down the passageway
Entering the carrier, designed to take them to their goal.

Doors are shut, safety instructions given
The voice of the Captain outlines the trip ahead.
Luggage stored, seatbelts buckled, we feel movement.
On the runway, engines revved to full power.
Tension feels relief, as we leave the ground to soar into the sky.
Leaving the Airport to others, waiting in pods, for their call to come.

Berlin

Berlin, Germany is a city once divided, after conflict
Caused by dreams to conquer, of evil men.
The suffering now a memory of days gone by
When freedom was lost to all. Many disappeared
Murdered for their background or beliefs, a terrible tragedy.
A field of concrete-like coffins memorial to the Jewish Holocaust.

Today tourists flock to view the many sites of the past
Walking down the Unter Den Linden to the Brandenburg Gate ,

Reminder of the hated Berlin Wall, which divided Germany
 in half.
Cutting off all contact between neighbours, friends and
 family.
Hundreds lined up, each day, to visit the Reichstag building
Where once the forces of evil prevailed.

Now free to travel and enjoy the sights and sounds of Berlin,
We notice the happy attitude displayed by the German
 people
Ready to welcome us and share food, entertainment and
 music.
A country where masters ,Mozart, Strauss and many others
Provided the world with music that pleased the
 connoisseurs.
A city rising like the phoenix, free as it ought to be.

The Polar Bear Express

At the end of the rail in the northern land
Many await the arrival of the mighty engine
Pulling cars, with mail, people and provisions
For the settlement of Moosonee and beyond
Passing several villages of the Cree Nation
Trappers, hunters and fishermen, bound to support families
From the fruits of the land, a proud people, surviving.
By their will, labouring freely for their preservation.

When the Polar Bear Express, so aptly named,
Arrives in Moosonee, an anxious group of people wait.

Travel Observations

Hoping to hear from friends or family, so far away.
Looking also to meet those who venture north,
Having personal desires as tourists or natives, come to visit
This land of beauty so unlike their family homes.

In Winter, the bitter winds and snow prevail.
The river in deep freeze supports trucks, horses and dog teams,
Their drivers racing across the frozen wastes,
Transportation for provisions or to visit their trap lines,
The source for meeting their daily needs.
Life is not easy, dressed in heavy parkas, mukluks on feet,
Deerskin gloves, to warm hands as mercury plunges
To 60 degrees below zero, chilling them to the bone.

When summer does arrive, for a few short months,
Crops show a rapid growth unlike in the south,
Responding as if the earth knows that soon the frost will come
When once again the land begins to cool.
Then, at night, the Northern Lights hang in the sky like curtains
Changing colours, bringing delight to all who observe
The warmer season, filled with pests and flies
Soon disappears when bitter cooler days resume control.

Those who venture to visit northern climates
Must share the thrill of the train to Moosonee,
Then riding in a freight canoe, across the river Moose,
To the village of Moose Factory, home of the Cree,

Centre of trading at the company of Hudson's Bay.
Seals are often seen cavorting in the river, while geese fly above
Children laughing, family dancing, men gone trapping.
A community of happy souls, in their chosen place.

The train connects the north to southern towns and cities,
Winding its way from Cochrane, then back again.
Providing the only meansfor reaching many people,
Separated only by distance, in the forest.
A nation spread over countless miles
Proud of their heritage, and their tribal lands
Living, by choice, outside the realm of modern advances,
Able to connect, only when riding the train.

The Canadian

Slowly the train crawled out of Toronto, travelling
From the Great Lakes toward the Pacific Ocean
Bearing a mixture of humanity from many cultures
All seeking to reach their chosen destinations
Passing by many types of habitations,
Towns, villages, and hamlets along the way.
Whistle sounding, to warn the people of their presence
For the sake of safety, all must clear the way
To allow the journey; continue without delay.

Lakes suddenly appear, with cottage on the shore,
Retreat for those who labour in the city,
Embracing nature, in its rarest form

Travel Observations

Detached from urban realities
Surrounded by the beauty of creation,
Aware, this paradise did not just appear,
'twas formed by the omniscient Hand of God.
Many miles of forest, trees growing close together,
Scenes quickly changing, to the delight of all aboard

On reaching the Prairies, the land lay flat for miles
Fields producing wheat for daily bread,
Monster machines, gathering harvest, to feed the world,
Manitoba, Saskatchewan move slowly past our windows,
Something of a sameness, lacking variety.
On to Alberta, where oil rises from deep below,
To permeate the sands, for man to find,
While in the north, the logging industry
Converting trees into lumber, used to build.
Man's venture into sharing God's creation.

Slowly, physical changes are apparent.
Hills begin to rise on the landscape,
Then Mountains, in all their majestic beauty,
Rise up to heaven, with their caps of white,
Proudly reaching to their highest point
A sight to match, the Wonders of the World.
Trees cannot live in the higher levels
Rocks rise above to claim their proper name
The Rocky Mountains, stand firm forever.

The train, descending, through the mountain pass,
River flowing by, towns and cities come in view,

Entering the way to the great Pacific Ocean,
Ever closer to the gem of pleasant living, Vancouver.
A vibrant bustling city Home of many races
Determined to be the finest Olympic venue on earth.
Our trip has brought us through so many vales
Our thanks to those who labour every day
For tourist and traveler, super meals and comfort
We salute the Canadian, an experience to be remembered.

Afternoon in English Bay (B.C.)

Sitting on a beach, on a gorgeous September day,
By the beautiful shore of English Bay,
Dwellers of Vancouver, enjoying the sun,
Before colder days will most surely come
An unexpected treat from the Lord up above,
Couples, joined with one they truly love.
Birds of all sorts, cover the beach,
Seagulls and pigeons, large numbers of each,
Then, of a sudden, a flock of Canada geese appear
Strutting their stuff, with no sign of fear
While out on the Bay, merchant ships mark their place,
Having crossed the Pacific, they now show their face.
A mixture of goods and cultures descend,
Arrayed on the ocean, in numbers, no end,
Waiting to unload their cargo on shore.
Sun beaming down warming people some more,
Waves from the ocean, gently caressing the sand,
A day to remember, peace and joy in our land.
Thanks be to our God, who blesses our days

Be thankful and answer, giving Him praise.
When the rain may arrive, as most surely it will,
No complaints will apply, that the sunshine won't kill
So let us be joyful, for such beauteous days
In chorus our thanks and assent we must raise,
A time to remember, as out to sea we gaze.

Winter in Moose Factory (James Bay) 1946

Set in the midst of the mighty Moose River
An island is home to many people of the Cree Nation.
Having daily needs for food and shelter,
Provided by their men, who hunt and fish for a living,
Houses built by the Fur trader, the Company of Hudson's Bay
For families of trappers, gone to the bush to seek their prey
Returning with their catch of fox and beaver pelts, to trade
At the Company store for food and provisions
Life was not easy tor those who hunt trap and fish
To earn their daily bread in such a clime.

In winter, the sun shines brightly on the ice and snow.
As dog-teams work, pulling their sleds to their goal,
The native driver, giving them direction,
"Huic! Huic!" they cry, urging their dog team forward,
Crossing the River Moose to Moosonee,
Dogs straining together, to provide transportation,
Threading their way, past small islands, across the river ice,
They cross the frozen river, in quick time, while, at night,
In the sky, the Northern Lights hang like curtains
Changing colours, as they pulse, in the Northern sky.

Riding outside, on a company truck. the trapper stands
With bronze-like face, facing the brutal wind and zero weather
Showing no signs of weakness from the cold,
Part of the proud Cree Nation, child of the heroes of long ago.
Today, dressed in heavy parka, hood off head, deerskin gloves
While mukluks are worn to cover feet and legs.
So he arrives in Moosonee, to meet the train, the Polar Bear Express
The link, by rail for those who dwell in the deep forest.
Eight months of winter keep air fresh and cold.
Until the river ice begins to move, down to the Bay named James

From the Abitibi River, into the Moose River and on to James Bay
For days, large masses of ice pass by the factory island,
Carving portions of land away from the shores of the island.
Paths where lovers walked washed by force, down the river.
A change in seasons, noticed by the coming of flies, mosquitoes.
Bulldog flies and no-see-ems, small but able to inflict pain to humans
Summer comes quickly and crops mature in very short time,
Bringing some relief, before the signs of winter return in early September.

Part 4

Poems on Various Subjects

Night Time (On the Farm)   71

The Coming of Spring   71

Summer   72

Little Bug   73

Thunderstorm   74

Rain Barrel   75

Lone Diner   76

Singles Dance   77

Grade 10 English Class   78

Age and Youth   79

The Mind   80

Back to School Trilogy #1 — The Parent   81

Back to School Trilogy #2 — The Teacher   82

Back to School Trilogy #3 — The Student   83

The Hands of a Man   83

The High School Resource Room   85

Loneliness   86

Homeless in the City   87

Dandelion   89

Philosopher's Walk (University of Toronto)   90

The Rush of Life   91

Short Visit   93

End of Summer   94

Night Time (On the Farm)

The clock is slowly ticking the hours away.
A moth is buzzing about my dismal room,
While over the meadow, the moon is beaming right,
As the sounds of the farm grow still in the silent night.

Gone is the chirp of the robin that thrilled me by day.
Still is the scramble of feet, cross the hardwood floor.
All have departed, leaving me here in the cold,
Alone and uncared for, a sheep of the Master's fold.

When the last tender hours, have passed away from my sight,
Will the tapering seconds lead darkness to thicker doom?
Ah! But nay, in the dark is a brightness that's shining for aye.
'Tis the light of my Saviour, burning to show me the way.

The Coming of Spring

A movement on my patio; what was that?
A small black squirrel, searching for his food,
To fill his empty belly, after long winter sleep.
Climbing trees, running on the fence top.
Eyes darting, to and fro, examining his waking world.

A call from high above, a crow being heard,
Announcing the change of season. "Caw, Caw,"
He shouts, "Where are the other birds from south.
Building nests, and laying eggs, for me to eat"

Receding snow reveals a brown carpet.
Covering the earth, frozen by days of winter,
Now warming in the sunshine, green shoots appear,
Proclaiming the coming, of another Spring,
Awakening thoughts of Love in girl and boy.

The messages of change are all around,
Out of the darkness, comes the longer light of day
Under the sun, cold winter fades away.
Rain from heaven, gently feeds the grass and flowers
The hearts of men are thankful and refreshed,
By all the signs of warmer days ahead.

Summer

Summer's here, right as rain
Warmer days have come again,
Birds in trees, worms on ground
Beaches crowded, no parking found
Crowded highways, city exodus
Picnics, jogging, fun for all of us
Water sports fill the bay,
Swimmers, water-ski, sport of the day.
Football, baseball, in the park
Lovers, smooching after dark.
Time to light the barbecue
To share with friends, like me and you.
Days of sun, with loads of heat
Hot dogs, ice cream, food to eat
Hope these days will never end

Walks on trails with closest friend.
If choice was given for time of year
Most votes would go to stay right here
A time to play, a time to love,
Give thanks for this to Lord above.
For joys received when days are warm,
Oh dear! I think I hear a storm.
The heavens grow dark, the sky lights up
To shelter go, no time to stop
A shower or two, then back to sun,
Rejoice my friends, for summers come.

Little Bug

While resting on my patio, one warm Spring day
A little bug flew in and landed on my table
Walking about, taking possession of his turf
Asking himself, why he had come this way?
Discovering a world, like none he had known,
Exploring the surface, as if to make it his own.

His search gave nothing good to eat.
No reason here to stay, he thought,
When plants and flowers, growing all around,
Gave hope for treats, most tasty, to be found.
Spreading out his wings, away he flew
Leaving me with other things to do.

Thunderstorm

The heavens were dark as clouds rushed by,
A streak of lightning split the sky
Roar of thunder, shattering the quiet
The storm was here to stay, no one dare deny it.
As rain poured down without relief
Robbing our sunny day, a sudden thief.

A break in clouds, a ray of sun shone through.
From out its nest, a bluebird quickly flew.
Taking a chance to seek its daily bread
Despite the black clouds forming overhead.
Once more the storm in all it's fury broke,
With light and sound to scare the common folk.

Results were dire as nature ruled the sky,
Restricting all birds from their nest to fly.
Pelting rain on trees and windows fell,
An end to this we could not really tell.
It seemed the world was hidden from the sun,
We wondered if the end of life would come.

We remember Noah, who fashioned the Ark
To house men and species as the world grew dark,
When God sent the flood to cover the earth,
To destroy all the evil and those of no worth.
When the flood ended, was born a new nation,
A plan for preservation of civilization.

Today we search clouds for the sign of the bow,
Shining bright in its colour, brings peace to below
The promise to Noah, rebounds in our life.
God's rainbow promises safety from strife.
It has been ordained, that man should survive.
The promise shows Love to keep us alive.

Rain Barrel

The rain fell gently on the roof of the shed,
Collecting in the evestrough, it poured,
Into a barrel, where it could be saved.
"Soft water" it was called, perfect for certain use.
Washing hair and clothes, made the soap go further,
Avoiding the harshness of tap water,
Warmed by the sun on summer days, pure from heaven
Clothes washed in rainwater, with a gentle soap
Seemed so soft and comforting, worn in days gone by.

Modern living has forgotten the use of rain barrels
Filled with water, the tears of a clouded sky,
Rich in quality, replaced by chemical means of living,
Seeking a sterile environment for our children.
Attempts to better nature, by our knowledge,
Building walls, we isolate ourselves from natural solutions
Replacing gifts of creation, with lab developed prescriptions,
The healing powers of nature shunned by modern science,
Consigning past solutions, such as rain barrels, to our memory.

When customs of the past have all been put to rest,
When nature has no place in healing practice,
When Pills have full control, in keeping us alive,
Can we rejoice, knowing we have the secrets to prolong life
Or will this new world, begin to give way to remedies forgotten,
Administered by those who find old secrets from the past.
Challenging the plastic world of modern science and research,
Man may wake to the truth that not all things past have little use,
Things discarded may return, even the very useful old rain barrel.

Lone Diner

Sitting alone in a restaurant,
Mind filled with memories
Of better days, sharing with one, so loved.
Life is difficult, faced with decisions,
Wishing for the hand of a friend,
But, alas, forced to dine alone.

Families and friends, at nearby tables
Conversations mixed with laughter
Sharing delight at being together
Joined in common purpose.
Food, to satisfy their bodily needs,
Bonds of Kin and Friendship holding fast.

Pleasant servers come to take my order,
Showing interest, taking time to chat.
Brief exchange of comment eases tension.
The lone diner observes the present scene
With some sense of being a central part.
The total group around me gives me peace.

Singles Dance

Slowly the crowd arrived, to join the group of adults.
Many, like they, single, divorced, separated, lonely souls
They filled the hall, seating themselves at tables.
Looking for company, failures in Love, seeking a second chance
Hoping this night would be the answer to their needs.

The bar was busy, serving drinks to all who had the cash
Looking to feel the effects of alcohol on their bodies,
Allowing some to be relaxed, while others enter a quiet mode.
Like shy students, at a high school dance,
Wanting closeness but hesitant to make the first move.

The night wore on, as music took control.
Inviting all to dance to loud refrains,
The floor became a stage of pulsing bodies
Moving to the strains of blaring speakers.
Too loud to permit meaningful conversation
For those who needed to share stories and ideas.
Some sat watching, not joining in the fun and games,

Until the hours passed, and tired bodies filtered out,
Ending the night, they sought only to reach their homes
Anxious to return to solitude, in the arms of Morpheus.

Grade 10 English Class

A group of students, assembled together,
Attendance taken, assignments given,
Work to be completed; in preparation
For a life, facing a complicated world,
Success or failure, a future possibility.

Plugs in ears, listening,
To musical devices, designed to entertain;
Never intended to aid in education
Explained by some as part of multi-tasking
In reality, an interference in the learning process.

Some students, making progress
Facing the challenge of directed tasks
Seeking to do as asked, slowly improving,
The light of learning, shining through their eyes
Lives seeking knowledge, for their future.

Boys and girls, brought together by age and performance,
Trying to make the most of this experience,
Efforts to follow the teacher's guidance;
Or attempts to disrupt the field of study
Both groups, doing daily, what appeals to them.

To observe a class striving to advance
Many personalities, competing at a common task
Questions arise as to the future of mankind.
Will we see a nation, determined to make a better world,
Or will disaster prevail, caused by those who fail to learn.

Age and Youth

Age leads one to a much clearer perspective,
Providing the urge to be more directive.
Assuming that knowledge can be transmitted,
To much younger people, not fully committed.
Making their choices without time to wonder
What may transpire, to cause them to blunder,
Blindly choosing the joy of the minute,
No consideration given, to see what is in it,
We plan without care, for those wiser than we,
Hoping my world will be better for me.
The adventures and experiences, learned in life,
Can soothe us in comfort, or cut like a knife.
So we walk boldly forward, living our plan,
To be the loved woman or the capable man.
Learning as we go, becoming the best we can be,
Ignoring the knowledge, from our family tree.
Life passes so quickly' till one day we know,
We now see so clearly, our perspective does grow.
As we arrive at the point where our elders were to us,
We now try to help those younger, without any fuss.
But they cannot hear, too busy choosing their way
Passing us off as advice from yesterday.

Our wisdom is lost, to give help to the young.
They will not comprehend, until their journey is done.

The Mind

The mind is a vessel, beyond all compare
Storing knowledge in bits, gained from everywhere
Beginning at birth, as experiences are found
From exposure to people, where memories abound.
We learn to talk, by listening to others,
Siblings and friends, but mostly, our Mothers.
Habits and traditions become an art,
As the mind uses memory to set us apart.
Reaching to grasp the truths, vital for life,
While our bodies mature, and we battle with strife
Using the know-how, ingrained in our mind,
The future begins to look rosy, we find.
Until, one day as an adult we discover
Problems appear, unlike any other.
We meet with a person, we've known really well,
But where we had known them, we can't really tell
A glitch in the system, appears to have been made
When time and place change, our abilities fade.
So many bits are stored in our brain
But alas, in our search, we fail to attain.
The longer we live, the more info is stored
To find a solution we may often get bored.
The simple mind works for its owner, the best
Too much information, seems, our mind to arrest
So, thanks be to God, for what he has given

A vessel to serve us, until we reach Heaven.
It may lack perfection, but better than nought
"Now what was that name? O dear, I forgot"
Our mind serves us well, for most of our days,
Without it, we're lost, lie a soul in a daze.

Back to School Trilogy #1 — The Parent

Tears in her eyes she waves goodbye to her child
Knowing a change would be seen so very mild
But, slowly would mould her little one,
As her education was now begun.
Homework to help with, lunches to make,
Meetings with teachers, worries lead to headache.

As time quickly passes and bodies do grow,
New challenges for parents, wherever they go.
Parties and dances, young men come calling
Daughters impressed, hard to keep from falling
Teenage experiences, provide new worry,
As they try to grow up in such a big hurry.

School seems to be the least of parent concerns
Keeping them on track, from suffering burns.
The trials of parenting seem never ending
While daughters debate, their virginity defending
A difficult time, that may only subside,
When a marriage takes place, and they all glow with pride.

Life as a parent is filled with trial and error,
'Tis good that in couples, there's someone else to care for.

Back to School Trilogy #2 — The Teacher

Freshly trained, anxious to start,
She entered the school, with rapid beating heart,
Soon to face challenges, in her first class
The teacher walked boldly, with knowledge to pass.

A group seated, waiting, to see who would come,
Anxious to learn, but also have fun.
They welcomed her loudly, when first she appeared,
Hoping this person was not to be feared.

As the teaching began, a bond was soon formed,
New learning took place, they became more informed
Slowly, days turned to weeks, ending the term.
A career begun, showed success to confirm.

Year after year, the task was repeated
Classes came and went as their tasks were completed,
The teacher was honoured for her years of success
When her last day approached, she could finally rest.

Her career was ended, she looked back with pride
At the many fine students, who had worked by her side,
Discovering knowledge to last them forever
Her work now done, she found great pleasure.
She was thankful for events that led to her career
Her memories would please her for many a year.

Poems on Various Subjects

Back to School Trilogy #3 — The Student

The small boy timidly approached the large building.
Having left his mother at the edge of the schoolyard
He slowly walked up the steps and into a new phase of his life
Now the learning would begin, to prepare for his future
A new world, unlike his early years of freedom.
Running through fields, finding treasures in the outdoors,
Worms, frogs, butterflies, ants, flowers, trees.
Exchanged for long periods of sitting, searching in books.
His years passed slowly as he yearned for former freedom,
But his mind was inspired by new challenges,
So many areas of study, opening a new world.
The child who had begun the journey was transformed.
His education had prepared him for the adult world
No more regrets of his lost childish freedom.
He strolled resolutely into a phase able to choose his destiny.

The Hands of a Man

As life draws slowly towards the end
Hands reach out to embrace a friend.
Time has taken its toll on body parts,
Now showing wear from ambitious starts.
The eyes now dim, the joints grown stiff
Teeth now replaced by modern art.
The legs slow down, arthritic in part.
Each suffer the many ravages of living,
Working each day, forever giving
All they can, as they are able
In effort to keep the body stable.

Hands have a special place in life,
When holding the hands of a child or wife
A history of growth, from the very start;
Reaching to grasp each precious part
The child may have a cat to love a dog to pet
Learning to write, a computer to set,
Piano to play, dishes to wash.
Windows to clean to make the home posh
Multiple tasks, our hands called to do
Household chores, community work too.

When a man considers the work of his hands
The memory speaks to his life in the land
Riding a bike, batting a ball, apples to pick, painting a wall
Friendly fights, waving to friends, fixing toys, standing tall,
Holding baby, lest he fall, secure in loving hands
So many ways our hands do serve us,
We lift them up in praise to God above
And offer a hand in showing friends our love.

Our hands serve us well for all our earthly tasks
From milking cows to lifting high a glass.
For shoveling snow, or pulling child on sled,
A list unending, so it may be said.
Our hands should aid us when helping others,
Family and friends, with problems that tend to smother
Giving a hand to all the less fortunate
Completing our destiny, in a task most important
For the hands of Creator, who fashioned the earth
Provided potential for men and women from birth

So our reason for being, will surely be done
When we offer our hands, the victory is won.

The High School Resource Room

Deep in the heart of the School Community,
A room exists where students come for help.
Needs of individuals are met with love and concern
By persons, who with knowledge and resolve
Labor daily to provide the right directions.
Assistants in the task of education.

Assignments to complete, work left undone,
Information sought and given, work completed
Some writing tests, others sent by teachers
To test this venue, hoping students will respond
In a place of relatively unstructured learning
So daily they assemble to face individual tasks.

Mixture of youth, bound by common purpose.
Unseen motivation, strongly affecting actions taken.
Parents to please, teachers demanding real results,
This inner self looking to reach levels of achievement
A struggle designed to prepare for future ventures
Touching societal needs for useful living.

Capable, empathetic, trained educational assistants
Make possible a chance for many to reach success
Friendly, accepting treatment works a miracle
Students, with little hope show great response,

The system works for many who are lost
Caught by the Spirit of learning, they begin to cope.

Loneliness

They come from every walk of life.
Alone, they face a world designed for sharing by many.
Lives, doomed to solitary existence, not of their own choosing.
Seeking one to share the joys and sorrows of a troubled world.
Products of families, where once they lived together and loved,
Celebrating special moments, on life's journey, with their kin.

Time wreaks change, experience shapes the individual.
Paths may lead to scenes, devoid of former comforts.
Failure in marriage, forced to walk an unfamiliar street.
Changes in habits, consigning the past to memories.
Some, used to single living, others confused by new directions.
Having dealt with crowds in early days, now reduced to solitary state.

Loneliness is a blight on life, leading to the death of lively spirit.
Coming silently, surrounding its victims, like a spider's web,
Holding firm a soul, that only cried for love and friendship
Rejected at every turn, losing contact with all. The power of silence

Enfolds the soul, closing all doors that might have led to freedom
Binding the lonely, in a tomb of shattered dreams.

How do they exist, without their basic needs supplied ?
Some turn in panic to their God, Peace from prayer and meditation
Others continue to search for one they may never meet.
Happy the soul who finds a friend, caring, expressing love. Sharing
The joy of life, giving hope to the lonely, making living bearable.
Providing comfort and warmth, by words, and acts of kindness.

In a crowded world, people of every creed and colour,
Face unknown challenges, like roadside bombs, meant to try them.
The fortunate, share family joys, and the love of good friends,
While others, lead lonely, troubled lives with little comfort.
We find the answer to the needs of mankind, by offering care and love
By sharing with all living, Peace and friendship, to end loneliness.

Homeless in the City

Seated at a street corner in a large city,
Dirty, unshaved, dressed in ragged clothing,
Seeming not to notice the rain falling all around;

A body ravaged by weather, his features drawn,
His life's belongings, stuffed into an old potato sack.
A life all but lost, slowly deteriorating over time.

How came this person, to such a pitiful state?
No one would have imagined, life ending in this way.
His eyes were dull, reflecting little future hope.
Yet once, his face showed promise, striving for success,
Making good business deals, reaching for the moon.
But now he sits helpless, having lost hope, as others took his place.

His fall from grace was tragic, from choices wrongly made.
Wife and children had depended on his actions.
His loving wife, neglected, his children abandoned
As he walked down new avenues, tempted by impure thoughts.
He sought love and success, in all the wrong places
Rejecting all the people and tasks that had led to a bright future.

Strong drink and use of drugs wrought havoc in his life
Unable to maintain his home, he walked away leaving pain behind.
Employers found no reason to keep him in his job.
He left with no place to lay his head, no family, no job, no friends.
Life was brutal, the result of the choices he had made
So he became the street person we found on that corner.

As years passed by, his life could be no better,
Living on the street, accepting coins and scraps from strangers,
Sleeping on subway grates for warmth on bitter cold winter nights
No joy for this person, suffering from his own selfish choices.
One day a bright young man passed by, shocked by the sight
Of this wretched bearded person who seemed vaguely familiar

No, he thought this could not be the father who deserted our family
The creature seemed much too old, heavily bearded, in ragged clothes
The young man left, feeling no connection to this derelict.
His father knew now, the pain he had caused. Wanting it all to end
He reached for the drug, hidden in his pocket, seeking to find release
Softly he said "I'm sorry ", as taking the potion, he slipped into oblivion.

Dandelion

Admiring the manicured green lawn, one summer day,
The country club member, had come, some golf to play.
Sudden surprise, shocked the player at what he saw,
A yellow flower was reaching up through the luscious grass.
How came this intruder to settle there, an act most crass.

Nature creates a scene, defying our most careful plan
Storms and wind together act, with no concern for man.
When day turns dark, deep waves roll, and lightning strikes
The world is changed by forces beyond our control.
Like mice that beat retreat, to their protective hole.

A seed from far away, carried by the soft summer breeze,
Had reached the ground one rainy day to rest in ease,
Hidden in the deep green grass it rooted and took its place.
Growing close to ground, unnoticed, doing its duty.
Until one day it raised its head, in all its glorious beauty .

The grounds man was engaged to deal with the situation,
No chance would be allowed for the flower at this station.
A common weed in a country club lawn would be destroyed.
The act was swift, the head chopped off, the root pulled out.
It had be done, no time for doubt, the threat was put to rout.

How simple it seems to get rid of the little dandelion.
In our perfect world, we think the result is fine.
But what of threats more serious to our way of life.
Until we find a way to deal in love with situations we deplore,
Our life remains, with need to grow until we learn much more.

Philosopher's Walk (University of Toronto)

And so they pass, while I in loneliness
Gaze down and up and ponder,
At life punctuated by silence

While traffic roars and heels click
On the walk beneath my window.

To whom the steps belong,
I do not know, or care, but listen,
To taps, coloured by laughter,
As stars wink, and clouds glide
In the sky above my window.

The flicker of a match,
Lights up a face in some dark corner,
Then hurried footsteps strike against the concrete
To glide across the grass, toward that glimmer
For some strange pre-arranged rendezvous.

A laugh, a call, a sudden scream,
Then quietness once more,
As silence slowly creeps upon the walk
And so I leave it to its hidden secrets
Choosing to flee, into the arms of Morpheus.

The Rush of Life

The world is rushing, to get to Where?
No one seems to really care.
Cars and trucks that speed along,
Drivers, sure, they do no harm.
People hurry to make the next light,
Taking no time to do things right.
Souls obsessed by the thrill of speed,

Selecting "Fast", 'the way to proceed.
Decisions made, in split-second time,
Resulting in anger, or even in crime.
Man was created to nurture the world,
How can he succeed, caught up in the whirl.
Trees are cut down, where once forests stood
Animals left, without sources of food.
Resources are plundered, for want of the buck,
Coal and wood, hauled off, in gigantic truck
Rape of the land, for the riches of living
Taken away, without any thought of giving.
Places on earth, masses dying of hunger,
Vain women and men spend much to look younger.
The balance on earth has been badly upset.
Our daily goal drives us, to what we can get.
When lack of concern for the needy is rife,
We should ask ourselves, the true meaning of life.
Created by God, for all creatures living
A plan to sustain, by kindness and giving.
Man oft' fails to engage in working the plan
Selfish goals prevent us, doing what we can.
Speed is the factor that controls our success,
Pressures of circumstance give us much stress.
While deep in our souls, certain questions arise,
Where are we going? Please open our eyes.
If we have ears, please let us hear,
Our purpose in life, a future free of fear.
We must slow down and ponder, work to be done,
Prepare for the day when the Kingdom will come.

Acts of Love and Kindness, healing for many
Sharing personal gifts and wealth with any
Who suffer each day, while we live in wealth,
Forgetting the millions, without food or health.
Time must be spent in making things right,
Now is the hour to fight the good fight.
Hunger and poverty on earth be destroyed,
This is the challenge, mankind can't avoid.
When the day of judgment has finally come
We must give account of what we have done.
Rewards are eternal for all who believe, sharing
The gifts of our Creator, so loving and caring.
So choose your armor wisely, to face the evil one,
When the struggle is ended, the victory is won.

Short Visit

Time flies quickly, when visiting friends,
Where does it go? When it starts and ends
Moments so precious, can never repeat
A joy to behold, but quick to retreat.
So savour the time with those you do love,
When the hour comes to part, embrace what you have.
Perhaps life permitting, you'll meet once again,
Till then, live in peace, though you may suffer pain.
Treasure the memories, when two were together,
Friendship survives, no matter the weather.
The seasons may change, but thoughts will remain
Till the day surely comes that you'll meet again.

End of Summer

Summer days are almost past
Any one could be the last
Daylight shorter, nights so cold,
Fall is here, so I've been told.
Dewdrops sparkle on fading grass
Frost appears, but does not last
Squirrels are searching, food to store
For the days, when there is no more.
Birds begin to flock and fly,
Wings spread wide, we wonder why
Winds blow cold around their nest
Heading south will be their quest.
Beach deserted, by the young,
Back to learning, they have come
Forgetting pleasures, t-shirts, shorts
Planning to turn to other sports.
Football, hockey, skiing will be,
The joys that appeal to the young and free.
Signs of winter soon appear,
The final season of the year.
Anticipation fills our mind,
Knowing the future, we will find,
Spring and Summer, come once more
With all the pleasures we adore.
So, thanks for all! Have good cheer!
Until Summer returns, for another year.